# EASY COOKING .... THE ISLAND WAY

Ann Kondo Corum

*Press Pacifica, Hawaii*

Library of Congress Catalog Card.

Corum, Ann Kondo.
    Easy Cooking — the island way.

    Includes index.
    1. Cookery, Hawaiian. I. Title.
TX724.5H3C67          641.5         81-19981
ISBN 0-916630-24-2                AACR2

Copyright © Ann Kondo Corum 1982.

All rights reserved.

Manufactured in the United States of America by Delta Lithograph Company, 14731 Califa Street, Van Nuys, California.

Published by Press Pacifica, P.O. Box 1227, Kailua, Hawaii 96734.

# INTRODUCTION

This cookbook evolved out of a recipe book I made as a gift for my son, Ken, when he went away to college and had to live in an apartment. Using our family favorites and keeping in mind a college student's lack of cooking knowledge, I tried to select dishes that were nutritious, easy to prepare, and economical.

Ken's questions to me, such as "How do you boil a chicken?" and "How do you make gravy?" made me realize the necessity of a "helpful hints" section.

However, this collection will be useful not only to college students, but to all who want hassle-free, but tasty meals.

Main Dish Munchies, 1

Sandwich Island Specialties, 27

Desperation Dinners, 57

Sweet Stuff, 67

And Etc...., 83

Helpful Hints, 95

## PEPPERONI SOUP

*Nice and spicy, easy to make. This makes a meal with grilled cheese sandwiches.*
*A Sunday favorite with us.*

1 stick pepperoni (about 12 oz.)
1 large can whole tomatoes
½ tomato can of water
1  15 oz. can kidney beans
1 large onion, chopped
3 stalks celery, sliced
3 carrots, sliced
1 tsp. dry oregano
salt and pepper to taste

Slice pepperoni into thin slices and saute over medium heat. Add celery and onions; cook until vegetables are limp. Add tomatoes and water. Mash the tomatoes with a spoon. Add kidney beans and carrots. Season with oregano, salt, and pepper. Cook, covered, over low heat until the carrots are tender.    *Serves 6*

## LENTIL VEGETABLE SOUP

*This was a favorite when we lived in "cold weather country—California." We still enjoy it in Hawaii.*

1 large onion, chopped
1 clove garlic, minced
2 Tbsp. salad oil
3 carrots, sliced
2 stalks celery, sliced
½ tsp. chili powder
5 c. regular strength beef broth, or 6 beef boullion cubes dissolved in 5 c. water
1 c. dry lentils
1  15 oz. can stewed tomatoes (optional)
3-4 frankfurters, sliced
Parmesan cheese

In a 3-4 quart sauce pan cook the onion and garlic in oil until limp. Add the carrots, celery, and chili powder and cook 1-2 minutes. Add the broth and lentils. Cover the pan and simmer gently until lentils are tender (about 35 minutes). Cover and chill if made ahead.

To serve, add tomatoes and franks and heat. Sprinkle each serving with Parmesan cheese.

*Serves 4-6*

## QUICK BEEF CHOWDER

1 Tbsp. salad oil
1 green pepper, seeded and diced
2 (1 lb. 8 oz.) cans of beef stew
1 (1 lb. 8 oz.) can of Italian tomatoes
1 can condensed cream of celery soup
1 can whole kernel corn
2 Tbsp. instant minced onion
1 Tbsp. chopped parsley
½ tsp. salt
½ tsp. marjoram
1 bay leaf

Saute green pepper in oil over medium heat. Add remaining ingredients; cover and reduce heat. Simmer for 15 minutes.   Serves 6

*A good camping dish. Considering everything comes from a can, it is surprisingly tasty.*

## COMPANY STEW

3 lbs. stew meat (or buy a chuck roast and cut it up—cheaper)
3 large carrots, cut in chunks
1 large onion, cut in wedges
1 large can tomatoes (1 lb. 12 oz.)
½ c. wine
1 Tbsp. brown sugar
1½ Tbsp. salt
1 bay leaf
pepper to taste
1  10 oz. pkg. frozen peas

Mix all ingredients except frozen peas together in a large pan with a cover (the pan should be ovenproof). Cook in 300 degree oven for 5-6 hours. 15 minutes before serving, add the peas and return to the oven. Thicken stew, if desired, with flour mixed with water. (see page 11)   *Serves 6*

Note:   You may add any other vegetables such as green peppers, celery, turnips, or fresh mushrooms.

*This was one of my favorite dishes while going to college and raising a baby. It's a "put in the oven and forget it meal" that is tasty too.*

## EASY CHILI

1 lb. ground beef
1 large onion, chopped
1  15 oz. can tomato sauce
1 large can of small red beans or kidney beans
2 Tbsp. chili powder
salt and pepper to taste

Brown meat; add onion and cook until limp. Add tomato sauce, beans (including liquid), chili powder, salt, and pepper. Simmer 30 minutes. If desired, top each serving with grated cheddar cheese.    *Serves 4*

*Another favorite from my college days when time and money were scarce.*

## SPAGHETTI SAUCE

1 lb. ground beef
1 large onion, chopped
1 clove garlic, minced
1 can tomato soup
1 can tomato sauce (8 oz.)
1 can tomato paste (6 oz.)
1 Tbsp. Spice Islands spaghetti sauce seasoning
1 tsp. dry basil
salt and pepper

Brown beef. Add onion and garlic and cook until onion is limp. Add remaining ingredients and simmer, covered for 1 hour. Pour sauce over boiled spaghetti. Top with Parmesan cheese.   *Serves 4*

*I learned this one from my mother. It is easy to prepare and tastier than many restaurants' spaghetti.*

## PIZZA SANDWICH SPREAD

½ lb. ground beef
½ lb. mild Italian sausage, casing removed
½ tsp. dry oregano
1 clove garlic
1½ tsp. Worcestershire sauce
1 6 oz. can tomato paste
salt and pepper to taste
2 c. grated mozzarella cheese

Cook ground beef and sausage over medium heat until brown. Skim off fat. Add all other ingredients except cheese. Cook for 10 minutes. Reduce heat to low and add the grated cheese, stirring to mix in cheese. Remove from heat. Toast bread or buns. Spread mixture on toast and bake in 400 degree oven for 5 minutes. Sprinkle with Parmesan cheese.   Serves 6

Note: You may substitute 1 lb. ground beef for ½ lb. ground beef and ½ lb. sausage.

*Make this ahead of time and freeze it. Makes a good quick lunch or fast dinner.*

## ENCHILADA CASSEROLE

1 lb. ground beef
1  15 oz. can tomato sauce
1 pkg. Enchilada Sauce Mix
½ c. water
1 chopped onion
1 can corn
1 pkg. (12) corn tortillas, torn into quarters
1 block (about 12 oz.) grated cheddar cheese
1 small carton sour cream (8 oz.)

*This casserole is good to make for a crowd. It freezes well, so you can make it in 2 or 3 small pans if you are feeding only a few people.*

Saute ground beef and onion. Add tomato sauce, water, enchilada mix, and corn. Simmer 20 minutes. Grease 1 large pan or 2 small pans. Layer tortillas, sauce, sour cream, and cheese. Repeat, ending with the cheese. Cover with foil and bake in 350 degree oven for 45 minutes. Remove cover for last 5 minutes of baking time. Let stand about 10 minutes before serving.    Serves 8

Note:  This freezes well uncooked. Add 20 minutes to baking time if frozen.

## MIKEY'S MOM'S CHILI RELLENOS

*This is a short-cut version of Chili Rellenos that comes from Frances Mount, who is originally from Texas.*

2 cans whole green chilies
½ lb. sharp cheddar cheese, grated
1 pkg. Monterey Jack cheese, cut into strips
2 eggs
2 c. milk
½ c. flour
1 tsp. salt
Parmesan cheese

Drain chilies and remove the seeds. Put strips of Jack cheese into each chili. Beat eggs slightly; add milk, flour and salt. Place the chilies stuffed with Jack cheese in a 9 inch baking pan. Pour the egg-milk-flour mixture over the chilies. Add grated cheese and sprinkle top with Parmesan cheese.
Bake for 45 minutes at 300 degrees.  *Serves 4-6.*

## HUEVOS RANCHEROS

2 Tbsp. butter or oil
1 clove garlic, crushed
1 small onion, chopped
1  15 oz. can stewed tomatoes
1 small can diced green chilies
1 tsp. sugar
salt and pepper to taste
6 eggs
grated cheddar cheese

In a sauce pan saute the garlic and onion in melted butter or oil. Stir in tomatoes, chilies, sugar, salt, and pepper. Bring to a boil, then simmer for 15-20 minutes. Prepare eggs (poach, fry, scramble—2 eggs per person). Place eggs in a dish, spoon sauce over. Top with grated cheddar cheese.    *Serves 3*

*Serve with warm tortillas. Makes a good brunch dish.*

## MEXICAN CHEF'S SALAD

Break 1 head lettuce into bite size pieces

Toss with 8 oz. sweet tomato-based dressing such as Kraft Catalina

Crunch and add: 1 small bag of Doritos (taco or nacho flavor)

Brown: 1 lb. ground beef. Add to it: 1 15 oz. can of kidney beans (with its liquid). Season with salt, pepper, and chili powder. Simmer 10 minutes.

Just before serving, toss ground beef mixture with salad greens. Top with chopped onions, tomatoes, grated cheddar cheese, avocados, and sliced olives.   *Serves 4*

*This is our family's "Sunday Night Special." I wash and tear a head of lettuce and grate cheese the day before. Then after coming home tired after a day of playing, it is easy to brown the meat and just toss all the ingredients together.*

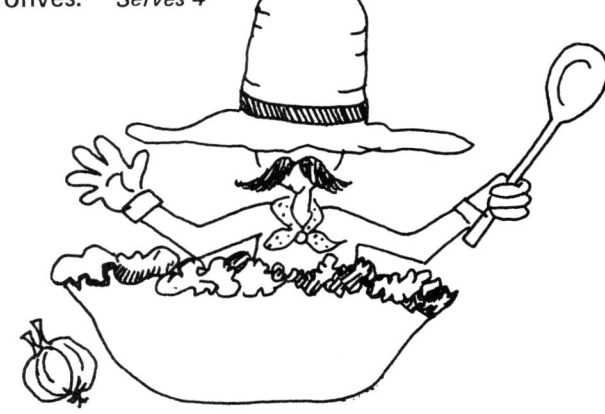

## MEXICAN CHICKEN CREPES

8 flour tortillas

Filling:
1 frying chicken, cooked. Remove skin and bones and shred meat

Add to chicken:
½ can cream of mushroom soup
½ c. sour cream
2 cloves garlic, minced
1½ tsp. chili powder
1 tsp. salt
1 tsp. cumin
1 small cane diced green chilies
10 oz. grated jack cheese
¾ c. sliced green onions

Spoon some chicken mixture onto tortilla. Roll up and place seam side down on greased baking dish. Bake, covered, in 375 degree oven for 25-30 minutes.

To serve:  Offer shredded lettuce, chopped tomatoes, grated cheddar cheese, and sliced olives to top crepes.   *Serves 4*

*Cook the chicken and allow it to cool overnight. It will be much easier to bone and shred.*

# CHALUPA

Cook 4 whole chicken breasts. Remove skin and bones and cut into bite size pieces. (A large whole chicken may be substituted for a more economical dish).
Cut 12 corn tortillas in quarters

Sauce:
1 can cream of mushroom soup
1 can cream of chicken soup
1 small carton sour cream
1 small can diced green chilies
2/3 c. milk
1 medium onion chopped
salt and pepper to taste
1 block (about 12 oz.) grated cheddar cheese

Mix all above ingredients together, except for the cheese. Grease a casserole dish or a 13 inch pan. Put in layers, the tortillas, chicken, sauce, and cheese. Repeat, ending with cheese on top. Bake, covered, at 350 degrees for 1 hour. During the last 15 minutes, remove the cover.

Note: You can easily make only half of this recipe . . . bake in an 8 inch pan for only 35 minutes.   *Serves 6-8*

*A very tasty recipe from Susan Larkey Corum, my sister-in-law in California.*

## CHICKEN DIABLE

*Super easy with an unusual taste.*

1 broiler-fryer cut up (or use chicken parts such as thighs)
½ stick butter or margarine
½ c. honey
¼ c. prepared mustard
1 tsp. salt
1 tsp. curry powder

Wash chicken; pat dry with paper towels.
Melt butter or margarine in a shallow baking pan large enough to hold all the chicken.
Add all other ingredients to the butter and stir. Roll chicken in the sauce to coat on all sides. Arrange in a single layer in the same pan.
Bake for 1 hour at 350 degrees, turning chicken once.

*Serves 3-4*

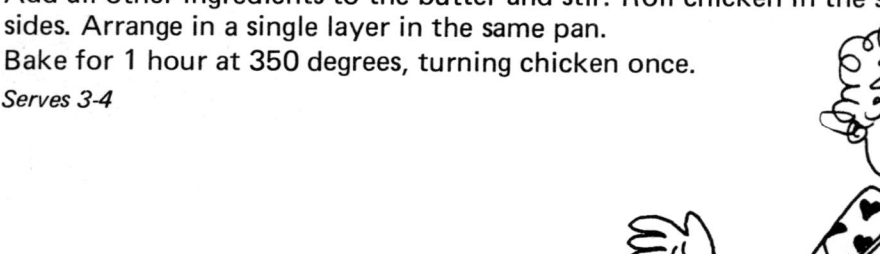

# EASY CHEESY CHICKEN

1 fryer chicken (or use chicken parts)
prepared bread crumbs or corn flake crumbs (about 2 cups)
½ c. Parmesan cheese
1 tsp. garlic salt
pepper
chopped parsley (optional)
1 block melted butter or margarine

Shake bread crumbs, cheese seasonings, and parsley in a bag.
Melt butter or margarine in a pan.
Dip chicken in melted butter and then coat with crumbs.
Place in a large baking pan, making sure pieces don't touch.
Bake for 1 hour at 350 degrees.   *Serves 3-4*

## BEER-BE-CUED CHICKEN

*Good excuse to buy a 6-pack when you know you shouldn't.*

1 cut up chicken
1 tsp. salt
1  12 oz. can beer
1 Tbsp. molasses
½ c. catsup
1 Tbsp. lemon juice
1 Tbsp. minced onion

Combine all ingredients and marinate chicken in sauce overnight. Grill outdoors over charcoal, or bake in 350 degree oven for 1 hour.
*Serves 3-4*

## MEAT LOAF

*Another recipe from Gràndma Kondo, this meatloaf is very moist.*

2 lbs. ground beef
1 can vegetable soup
1 small onion, chopped
2 slices bread, shredded
¼ c. catsup
1 egg
1 tsp. salt
¼ tsp. pepper

Mix all ingredients together. Pat into a loaf pan. Cover with foil and bake at 325 degrees for 1 hour. Remove foil and bake another 30 minutes.

Serves 6

## EASY POT ROAST

*A Grandma Corum favorite.*

3-4 lbs. chuck roast
1 envelope dry onion soup mix

Place roast on a large piece of foil. Sprinkle soup mix over the roast. Close the foil tightly around the meat. Place in a baking pan and bake at 325 degrees for 3-3½ hours, or until the meat is tender. Remove the meat from the foil.

To make gravy:
Drain the pan juices into a sauce pan. Add water if necessary to have 2 cups of liquid. To thicken, pour ½ cup water into a jar or covered container; add 3 Tbsp. flour. Shake well. The consistency should be like that of white glue. Add the flour-water mixture gradually to the pan juices until desired consistency is reached. Be sure to stir constantly to avoid lumps. Season with salt and pepper to taste. If you gravy comes out lumpy, pour it through a strainer.   *Serves 4-6*

## SHORT CUT BEEF STROGANOFF

2 lbs. round steak
1 can cream of mushroom soup
1 pkg. dry onion soup mix
1 c. water
2 Tbsp. catsup
1 c. sour cream
dash of pepper

Cut steak into thin strips. Brown in a skillet with a little butter. Add mushroom soup, onion soup, water, and catsup. Stir all ingredients together. Simmer 1½ hours, or until the meat is tender. Add sour cream and pepper just before serving.

*Serves 6.*

## MIKEY'S HAMBURGER STROGANOFF

½ c. minced onion
1 clove minced garlic
¼ c. butter
1 lb. ground beef
2 Tbsp. flour
2 tsp. salt
¼ tsp. pepper
1 8 oz. can sliced mushrooms
1 can cream of chicken soup
1 c. sour cream
2 tsp. minced parsley

*This dish is memorable because Ken prepared it as a welcome home dinner when I left him alone to fend for himself one summer. Recipe comes from pal Mikey.*

Saute onion and garlic in butter over medium heat. Add meat and brown. Add flour, salt, pepper, and mushrooms. Cook 5 minutes. Add soup and simmer 10 minutes. Stir in sour cream and parsley and heat throughly. Serve on rice.   *Serves 4*

## POPPING PEAS

*Super easy and economical.*

1 lb. ground beef
1 large can whole tomatoes (1 lb. 12 oz.)
1 pkg. dry onion soup mix
½ pkg. medium width egg noodles (uncooked)
1  10 oz. pkg. frozen peas

Brown beef. Add onion soup mix and tomatoes. Mash tomatoes with a large spoon. Add the egg noodles and cook until noodles are soft. Add the peas and cook for 10 minutes. Do not overcook the peas. They should be green and pop in your mouth.   *Serves 4-6*

## BAKED FISH

Fish fillets (about 2 lbs.)
juice of 1 lemon
garlic salt
pepper
1 c. mayonnaise
¼ c. finely chopped onion
bread crumbs

Squeeze lemon juice on fish. Sprinkle with salt and pepper.
Mix mayonnaise and chopped onion together; spread on fish.
Sprinkle with bread crumbs. Bake in 425 degree oven for 20-25 minutes.

*Serves 4*

## TUNA BURGERS

*High in protein, easy to prepare. A change from the old hamburger.*

2 cans tuna, well drained
¼ c. minced onion
¼ c. minced celery
1 c. bread crumbs
½ tsp. salt
¼ tsp. pepper
2 eggs
¼ c. mayonnaise

Mix all ingredients together and fry as you would hamburger patties.

Serves 4

## TUNA SOUFFLE

1 large can evaporated milk with enough regular milk to make 2 cups
4 Tbsp. margarine
5 Tbsp. flour
1 tsp. salt
¼ tsp. pepper
2 eggs, beaten
2 cans tuna, well drained
1 Tbsp. lemon juice
¼ c. finely chopped onion
1 Tbsp. minced parsley (optional)

Melt margarine over medium heat in sauce pan. Add flour, stirring constantly. Add the milk a little at a time, stirring to make a smooth sauce. Add salt and pepper and cook until thickened. Beat the eggs and then add to the sauce gradually. Add the remaining ingredients and pour into a greased casserole or a large loaf pan. Bake for 30 minutes in 375 degree oven.    *Serves 4*

*Dresses up the old can of tuna.*

## QUICK AND EASY KIM CHEE SALAD

1 small head cabbage: Cut up and toss with ¼ cup rock salt. Let stand about 15 minutes, tossing often. Lightly rinse and drain.

Dressing:
2 Tbsp. salad oil
1 tsp. sesame oil
3 Tbsp. vinegar
2½ - 3 tsp. sugar
¼ tsp. salt
1 tsp. sesame seeds, roasted and ground
½ - 1 tsp. cayenne pepper
1 small carrot, cut in julienne slices

Mix above ingredients with cabbage and toss well. Refrigerate and chill. *Serves 4 - 6*

*This recipe comes from a friend, Sharon Kim Venegas, who taught a Korean Cooking class at the University of Hawaii.*

# CHINESE SALAD

1 medium head lettuce or romaine, finely shredded
1 small bunch Chinese parsley (cilantro or coriander), chopped
1 small bunch green onion, chopped
1 small can water chestnuts, sliced
½ c. celery, sliced thin
1 whole chicken breast, cooked and shredded
½ pkg. fried Chinese noodles (available in Hawaii; elsewhere use canned Chinese noodles)

Dressing:
6 Tbsp. sesame oil (if unavailable, use salad oil plus 1 Tbsp. sesame seeds)
2 Tbsp. cider vinegar
1 tsp. salt
1 Tbsp. sugar

Wash and chill greens. Toss with chicken, noodles, and dressing just before serving. Sprinkle with sesame seeds.   *Serves 6*

## NAMASU (VINEGARED VEGETABLES)

*This is a Japanese salad.*

**Basic Sauce:**
¼ c. sugar
¼ c. Japanese rice vinegar (if unavailable, use cider vinegar)
¼ tsp. salt
1 piece (about 1 inch) ginger root, cut in slivers
Mix all ingredients well and marinate vegetables in it.

**Cucumber Namasu:**
Cut 2 cucumbers in half lengthwise.
Slice in thin diagonal pieces.
Place in a bowl and sprinkle liberally with salt. Set aside 10 minutes then squeeze out water, using cheese cloth or a thin dish towel. Add sauce.
Note:   Cooked shrimp, clams, abalone slivers, or raw fish may be added.

**Bean Sprout Namasu:**
Rinse 1 pkg. bean sprouts; cook in boiling water not more than 2 minutes. Drain and pour sauce over and toss gently. Garnish with sesame seeds.     *Serves 4-6*

## GRANDMA'S TAKUWAN

*Smells strong, but tastes good.*

Takuwan is Japanese pickled turnip.

5-6 turnips, peeled, sliced, and placed in clean jars.

Sauce:
¾ c. sugar
¼ c. vinegar
1 c. water
¼ c. salt
¼ tsp. yellow food coloring
1 red chili pepper, chopped (optional)

Boil all sauce ingredients together to dissolve the sugar and salt. Cool. Pour over the sliced turnips. Place jars in refrigerator. Ready to eat in 2 days.

## HAWAIIAN CREAM CHEESE SPREAD

*This will disappear fast at a party.*

8 oz. cream cheese
½ c. shoyu (soy sauce)
1 tsp. Worcestershire sauce

Make diagonal cuts in the cream cheese on both sides. Mix shoyu and Worcestershire sauce together and place in a plastic bag with the cream cheese. Tie the bag securely and place in a bowl. Refrigerate for a week or up to 3 weeks, turning occasionally. Remove cheese from bag and garnish with chopped parsley or chives. Serve with your favorite cracker.   *Serves 6*

Note:  Make several of these at a time.

# KOREAN BARBEQUE SAUCE

½ c. sugar
2/3 c. shoyu (soy sauce)
1 Tbsp. liquor (optional)
1 piece ginger, grated
1 clove garlic, crushed
2 Tbsp. sesame seeds
2 Tbsp. salad oil
2 stalks green onion, chopped

Shake all ingredients together in a large jar. Store in the refrigerator. Marinate meat, chicken or fish in this sauce, or brush on hamburgers. *Yield: 1 cup.*

*Koreans traditionally use this sauce on short ribs or thinly sliced pieces of tender beef.*

# FRIED RICE

Cook 1 cup rice and cool. (Or use leftover cold rice.)

3 strips bacon, cut up
1½ c. ham, leftover beef or pork, cold cuts, frankfurters, or Spam
1 egg
1 Tbsp. shoyu (soy sauce)
3 stalks green onion, chopped

Saute bacon. Add strips of meat or cold cuts to the bacon fat and saute. Turn heat to low and add the rice. Mix egg with shoyu and add to the rice and meat. Add the chopped green onions.     *Serves 4*

## ORIENTAL OMELET

4 eggs
2 Tbsp. water
½ tsp. salt
½ tsp. shoyu (soy sauce)
2 tsp. sugar
1 stalk green onion, chopped
1 Tbsp. oil

Mix all ingredients, except oil, together with a fork. Heat oil in an omelet pan or frying pan. Pour eggs into pan and cook over low heat until set. Fold over and cook for a few minutes until done. Cut into diagonal slices.   *Serves 3-4*

*Shoyu and sugar give a different flavor to the eggs. Good cold also.*

## SWEET SOUR CHICKEN (OR PORK, MEATBALLS, SHRIMP, OR FISH)

3-4 lbs. chicken, cut up
garlic salt
flour
oil for frying
Sauce:
½ c. sugar
½ c. chicken broth or 1 chicken boullion cube dissolved in ½ c. water
½ c. cider vinegar
3 Tbsp. catsup
3 Tbsp. shoyu (soy sauce)
½ tsp. salt

Sprinkle chicken with garlic salt. Roll in flour and brown in hot oil. Drain on paper towels. Place chicken in a large baking pan and pour half of sauce over it. Bake 20 minutes in 350 degree oven. Turn chicken over; pour remaining sauce over it. Continue baking 30 minutes or until chicken is done. Garnish with pineapple chunks before serving.

Note: This sauce may be poured over browned meatballs, cooked pork chunks, sauted shrimp, or fried fish for variation.   *Serves 4-6*

## SWEET SOUR SPARERIBS

Brown 3 lbs. spareribs, cut into pieces.

Sauce:
2 Tbsp. cornstarch
½ c. pineapple juice
½ c. cider vinegar
¾ c. brown sugar
1 Tbsp. shoyu (soy sauce)
½ tsp. salt
2 cloves garlic, crushed
1 piece ginger root (½ inch) crushed

Pour sauce over browned ribs. Cover and simmer 1-1½ hours, or until meat is tender.   *Serves 6*

*Dress this dish up with chunks of pineapple or a turnip cut in thick slices. Add to the ribs about ½ hour before serving.*

# SUKIYAKI

1 Tbsp. oil
1 lb. beef or boned chicken breast, sliced thin
1/3 c. sugar
½ c. shoyu (soy sauce)
¼ cup broth or water
1 c. bamboo shoots, sliced
½ block tofu, cubed
1 round onion, sliced thin
½ c. mushrooms, sliced
1 bunch long rice, softened in water and cut into 4 inch lengths (omit if unavailable)
2 c. spinach or watercress, cut in 1½ inch pieces
1 small bunch green onion, cut in 1½ inch pieces

Heat oil in skillet. Brown beef or chicken. Add sugar, shoyu, and broth. Add all other ingredients, except the green vegetables. Cook 2 or 3 minutes. Add green vegetables. Serve immediately with hot rice.  *Serves 4*

## BEEF OR CHICKEN WITH VEGETABLES

This is a basic recipe for stir frying meat with vegetables. You may use any kind of thinly sliced vegetable or combination of vegetables such as broccoli, string beans, bean sprouts, cabbage, onions, carrots, celery, tomatoes, etc.

Marinate ½ lb. thinly sliced beef or chicken breast in:
2 Tbsp. shoyu (soy sauce)
1 Tbsp. cornstarch
½ tsp. sugar
1 Tbsp. sherry or other liquor (optional)

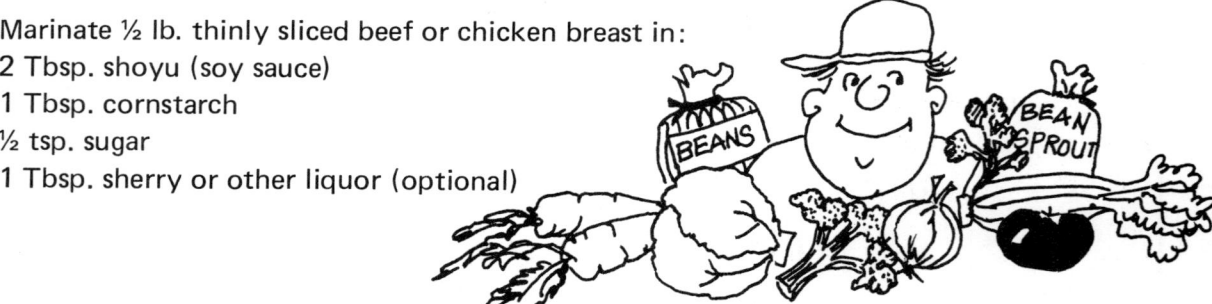

Heat some oil (enough to coat bottom of pan) in frying pan. Brown 1 clove crushed garlic and 1 piece crushed ginger. Remove from pan. Add beef or chicken and saute for 3 minutes, or until redness is gone. Do not overcook. Add thinly sliced vegetables and cook for only a few minutes. The vegetables should be crisp. Serve immediately with rice.   *Serves 3*

## MINUTE STEAK—ORIENTAL STYLE

1 piece of top round steak
salt
pepper
sugar
3 tsp oil
1 clove garlic, crushed
1 piece ginger, crushed
1 onion, cut in wedges
1 c. water
2 tsp. shoyu
1 Tbsp. cornstarch

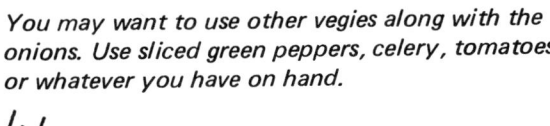

You may want to use other vegies along with the onions. Use sliced green peppers, celery, tomatoes, or whatever you have on hand.

Cut meat in serving size pieces. Then, with a sharp knife, slice through the meat horizontally so that the pieces of meat are about ¼ inch thick (easier to do if meat is partially frozen). Season meat with salt, pepper, and sugar. Heat oil in pan and saute garlic, ginger, and onion. Remove to a platter. Saute the meat, cooking only 1-2 minutes on each side (longer for well done). Place meat on the onions. Mix water, shoyu, and cornstarch together and add to the pan drippings. Cook until thickened. Pour over meat and onions.

# TERIYAKI CHICKEN OR BEEF ON A STICK

*Use basic teriyaki sauce from page 43*

Cut up 5-6 chicken breasts (boned) or cut up steak
1 box cherry tomatoes
2 onions, cut in wedges
2 green peppers or zucchini, cut in cubes
1 can whole mushrooms
1 can pineapple chunks

Marinate chicken or beef in teriyaki sauce for at least 1 hour. Drain pineapple and mushrooms. Cut up vegetables. Alternate meat, vegetables, pineapple, and mushrooms on skewers. Broil or barbecue over charcoal. Brush with any leftover marinade before serving.    Serves 6

*This is a standard dish we serve to our Mainland friends. It looks pretty; tastes good.*

## BAKED TERIYAKI CHICKEN

*Good to take on a picnic.*

5 pounds chicken parts

*Sauce.*

½ cup sugar
2/3 c. shoyu (soy sauce)
2 Tbsp. sherry or white wine (optional)
3 cloves garlic, mashed
1 inch piece of ginger, shredded (if unavailable, use 1 tsp. powdered ginger)
3 stalks green onion, chopped fine

Soak chicken in sauce overnight. Place chicken and some of the sauce in a large baking pan in 300 degree oven for 1½ hours, turning once.

This sauce may be used for steak also. Soak steak in sauce and broil. Leftover sauce may be stored in a covered jar in refrigerator.

Serves 6-8

## EASY PAN SUSHI

Cook 3 cups Calrose (Oriental) rice in 3 cups water. (See how to cook rice on p. 99). Put hot rice in a bowl and fluff it.

Vinegar Sauce:
½ c. Japanese vinegar (or cider vinegar)
½ c. sugar
1 tsp. salt
Heat sauce to dissolve the sugar. Cool.

Sprinkle half of sauce on hot rice. Toss gently with rice paddle or wooden spoon. Add more sauce to taste. Wet an 8 inch square pan. Shake off excess water; do not dry. Pack hot sushi rice into pan with wet fingers. Spread a piece of waxed paper or foil over pan and invert on a tray. Top with any of the following: colored shrimp flakes, tuna seasoned with teriyaki sauce (see p. 43), thin slices of takuwan (see page 32), cooked carrots cut in flower shape, or cooked shrimp.   *16 squares*

## TOFU PATTIES

Tofu is soybean curd; high in protein. It is available at Oriental markets and health food stores on the mainland and in all Hawaii markets.

Oil for frying
1 block tofu
½ c. cooked shrimp, chopped
½ c. carrots, minced
¼ c. green onions or chives, minced
2 tsp. sugar
1½ tsp. salt
2 eggs, slightly beaten

Blot excess water from tofu with paper towels; strain through a sieve or mash with a wooden spoon. Add the remaining ingredients and mix well. Make small patties. Heat oil in a skillet (about 2 Tbsp.) and fry patties until golden brown.   *Serves 4*

## SWEET SOUR TOFU AND VEGETABLES

1 block tofu
2 Tbsp. oil
1 c. sliced pork or chicken
1 clove garlic
1 slice ginger, crushed
1 c. broth or 1 boullion cube, dissolved in 1 c. water
3 Tbsp. shoyu (soy sauce)
¼ c. sugar
3 bamboo shoots, sliced
1 carrot, sliced thin
1 small onion, sliced
¼ c. Chinese peas (or frozen peas)
2 tsp. cornstarch
¼ c. water

Cut tofu in thick slices; drain on paper towels. Heat oil; saute pork or chicken with garlic and ginger. Add broth, shoyu, sugar, and vinegar and cook until meat is tender. Add vegetables and cook a few minutes. Add tofu slices. Thicken sauce with the cornstarch mixed with water. Serve with hot rice.   *Serves 4*

## MOCK LAULAU

Real laulau uses luau leaves (taro tops) and are wrapped in ti leaf bundles and steamed. This recipe is meant for those away from Hawaii.

¼ lb. (or more) salted butter fish or salted salmon
3 10 oz. pkg. frozen spinach, thawed and drained
3 or 4 lbs. pork butt, cut into large cubes
2 tsp. salt
pepper to taste

Soak salted fish in water for 1 hour. Drain and slice. Grease a covered casserole (or use pan and cover with foil). Layer spinach, pork, and fish. Season with salt and pepper. Bake, covered at 350 degrees for 1 hour or until pork is tender.    *Serves 8*

## OVEN KALUA PIG

4 lbs. pork butt
3 Tbsp. liquid smoke
2½ Tbsp. Hawaiian salt (or rock salt)
2 cloves garlic, crushed

*Any leftovers may be stir-fried with broccoli or cabbage sliced thin for another meal.*

Mix liquid smoke, salt, and garlic in a bowl and marinate the pork overnight. Wipe off the salt with damp paper towels. Place pork in a pan and cover with foil. (If you live where ti or banana leaves are available, wrap pork in leaves first). Bake at 350 degrees for 3-3½ hours or until done. Be sure pork is well done. Shred into bite sized pieces before serving.
*Serves 8*

# BEEF CURRY

2 Tbsp. oil
2 lbs. beef such as chuck, cubed
1 clove garlic
1 slice ginger or 1 tsp. powdered ginger
3 tsp. curry powder (adjust to taste)
2 tsp. salt
1 tsp. sugar
2-3 c. water
1 onion, cubed
2-3 stalks celery, cubed
2-3 carrots, cut in chunks
1 potato, cubed

Serve with condiments such as chutney, shredded coconut, chopped green onions, diced bacon.

Heat oil in heavy pan with a cover. Brown ginger, garlic, and beef. Add curry, salt, and sugar. Cook 3 minutes. Add water and bring to a boil. Lower heat; cook until meat is almost tender. Add vegetables and cook until soft but not mushy. Thicken sauce with flour mixed with water (see helpful hints . . . how to thicken gravy). Serve on hot rice.   *Serves 4-6*

## MOCK MALASADAS (PORTUGUESE DOUGHNUTS)

*What can be easier?*

1 roll refrigerated buttermilk biscuits
sugar
oil

Heat oil in a deep pan to 365 degrees (use electric skillet if you have one). Separate biscuits. Cook in oil until golden brown. Put some sugar in a paper bag. Shake hot biscuits in the sugar and serve immediately.  *Serves 4*

## GUAVA CRISPIES

**Crust:**
1 c. flour
½ tsp. salt
½ tsp. soda
½ c. brown sugar
½ c. butter
1 c. oats

**Filling:**
¼ c. butter or margarine
1/3 c. guava jelly
1 Tbsp. lemon juice
2 Tbsp. sugar
½ tsp. salt
1 egg yolk, slightly beaten

Mix together all ingredients for crust. Pat ½ of mixture in a 8 or 9 inch square pan.

Combine butter, jelly, lemon juice, salt, and sugar. Heat on low until jelly dissolves, stirring occasionally. Stir ½ of this mixture into beaten egg yolk, then return it to the jelly mixture. Heat until mixture thickens. Cool completely.

Spread jelly mixture on top of crumb crust. Top with remaining crumb mixture. Bake 25 minutes in 350 degree oven. Cut into squares.  *16 bars*

NOTE: Any flavor jelly or jam may be used.

*Sweet with an Island flavor*

## PINEAPPLE SQUARES

1 block butter or margarine
1 1/3 c. sugar
4 eggs
1½ c. flour
1 tsp. baking powder
½ tsp. salt
½ tsp. baking soda
1 no. 2 can crushed pineapple, drained
½ c. chopped macadamia nuts (may substitute walnuts)

Melt butter. Cream together butter and sugar with a portable electric mixer for 2 minutes on high speed. Add eggs; beat well. Add the dry ingredients. Add the pineapple and chopped nuts. Pour into a greased 9 x 13 inch pan and bake at 350 degrees for 30-35 minutes. Sprinkle top with powdered sugar and cut into squares.   *24 bars*

## MACADAMIA BUTTER BARS

1 c. butter or margarine
1 c. sugar
1 egg
1 tsp. vanilla
2 c. flour
1 c. chopped macadamia nuts

Cream together butter and sugar. Beat in egg and vanilla. Mix in flour and stir in ¾ cup of the nuts. Spread or press batter evenly into a greased 13 inch pan. Sprinkle rest of chopped nuts on top. Bake in 350 degree oven for 25-30 minutes. *24 bars*

## CITRUS PINEAPPLE LOAF

¾ c. chopped macadamia nuts
    (or almonds)
½ c. plus 1 Tbsp. sugar
½ c. butter or margarine
2 eggs
3 Tbsp. lemon juice
grated rind of 1 orange
1 8 oz. can crushed pineapple
3 c. flour
2 tsp. baking powder
½ tsp. baking soda
1 tsp. salt

Grease a 9 inch loaf pan generously. Sprinkle sides and bottom with chopped nuts and 1 Tbsp. sugar. Cream butter and sugar together until light and fluffy. Beat in eggs, lemon juice, and orange rind. Add undrained pineapple. Combine the dry ingredients and add to the pineapple mixture. Stir just until moistened. Pour into pan and bake at 350 degrees for 1 hour.

## CREAM CHEESE KANTEN

Kanten is a Japanese gelatin dessert made from agar-agar (seaweed). This is a simplified version.

1 8 oz. pkg. cream cheese
¾ c. sugar
4 pkg. Knox gelatin
½ c. water
1 c. 7-Up
1 c. juice from Mandarin oranges
2 c. Mandarin oranges (canned)

Cream the sugar and cream cheese together in a large bowl. Soften the gelatin in the ½ cup water. Add gelatin mixtue and all other ingredients, except the Mandarin oranges, to the sugar-cream cheese mixture. Mix well. Add the oranges last. Pour into a 9 x 13 inch pan. Chill until firm. Cut into squares.

Note: If Mandarin oranges are not available, use chunk pineapple. *24-36 squares*

## PINEAPPLE-BANANA SMOOTHIE

*This makes an excellent quick breakfast.*

¼ c. milk
1 banana, cut up
1 c. crushed pineapple
1 Tbsp. honey or sugar (optional)
1-2 Tbsp. high protein powder (optional)
2 ice cubes
handful of raisins or dates

Put milk, banana, pineapple, honey, and protein powder in blender and blend until smooth. Add ice cubes and raisins or dates and blend on high speed until ice is completely crushed.  *Serves 1*

Note:  Any fruit may be used in place of the pineapple. You may use oranges, mangoes, papaya, peaches, strawberries, etc. A large spoonful of peanut butter may also be added.

## CORNED BEEF HASH PATTIES

*Good for breakfast too!*

1 can corned beef
2 medium potatoes, diced
½ small onion, chopped
salt and pepper to taste

Cook the diced potatoes in water until soft (do not overcook). Drain well. In a bowl mix the potatoes, corned beef, and onions together. From
In a bowl mix the potatoes, corned beef, and onions together. Form into patties and brown in hot oil or butter in a frying pan.
Serve with fried eggs.    *Serves 3.*

## SCRAMBLED EGGS

For each serving use:

1 Tbsp. butter or margarine
2 eggs
½ cup milk
½ tsp. salt
pepper to taste

Break eggs into a small bowl.
Add milk, salt, and pepper and mix well with a fork.
Melt butter in a medium size skillet.
When butter is sizzling, pour in the eggs.
Lower heat immediately and stir the eggs constantly.
When eggs are set (but not dry), remove from heat.

You can add almost anything to scrambled eggs—ham or cold cuts, diced, chopped onion, grated cheese, herbs, parsley, mushrooms, etc.

## BEANIE-WEENIES

1 large can pork and beans.
¼ c. brown sugar
¼ c. catsup
2 Tbsp. finely minced onion
3 slices bacon (optional), chopped
3 hot dogs, sliced

Saute bacon over medium heat (if you do not have bacon, use 2 Tbsp. butter). Cook onion until it is limp. Add the rest of the ingredients and heat.   *Serves 2*

*Not exactly a gourmet dish, but it dresses up a can of beans!*

## CREAMED TUNA

1 can tuna
1 can cream of mushroom soup
½ small onion, chopped
½ c. milk

Stir all ingredients together.
Heat and eat! Serve on rice or toast. *Serves 2*

## TERI-HOT DOGS

Heat teriyaki sauce in a pan (see Teriyaki Chicken in Sandwich Islands Specialities section). Cut hot dogs in diagonal slices. Heat in teri sauce and eat!

*Adapt the amount you make according to your needs. For 1 serving use ½ cup sauce and 2-3 hotdogs.*

## CHICKEN NOODLE CASSEROLE

½ pkg. (or less) egg noodles
1-2 cans chicken (6½ oz. cans)
1 can cream of mushroom soup
1 Tbsp. minced onion (optional)
salt and pepper to taste

Cook noodles according to directions on package. Mix together the chicken, soup, onion, salt and pepper. Add the noodles. Pour into a buttered baking dish and bake in 350 degree oven for 1 hour.

Tuna may be substituted for chicken and macaroni may be used instead of noodles. *Serves 2 - 3.*

## SCRAMBLED HAMBURGER

1 lb. hamburger
1 small onion, chopped
salt and pepper to taste

Brown hamburger and onion in a little butter. Add salt and pepper.

A package of frozen peas or peas and carrots may be added if desired.

*Frozen hamburger can be used for this. Just cook it over low heat until it is thawed. Great "emergency" food.*

## CONFETTI CORNED BEEF

1 can corned beef
1 (10 oz.) pkg. frozen peas and carrots
½ small onion, chopped (optional)
salt and pepper to taste

Saute corned beef over medium heat in a skillet. Add peas and carrots and onions and cook until done, but not mushy. Season with salt and pepper.  *Serves 2*

## SKILLET HOT DOG DINNER

4 hot dogs, sliced diagonally
1 onion, sliced thin
1-2 potatoes, sliced thin
3-4 Tbsp. water
salt and pepper to taste

Saute hot dogs in a little butter or margarine. Add onions, potatoes and water
Cover and cook over low heat until the potatoes are soft. Season with salt
and pepper.
Serves 2.

# Sweet Stuff

# HEALTHY COOKIES

1 c. butter or margarine
½ c. brown sugar (packed)
1 c. flour
½ tsp. soda
2 c. old fashioned oats

Mix butter and sugar together until fluffy. Stir in flour, soda, and oats. Divide the dough in half. Form into rolls about 1½ inches in diameter. Wrap in waxed paper or foil. Chill at least 2 hours. Slice dough about ¼ inch thick. Place on ungreased cookie sheet and bake approximately 10 minutes.    *4 dozen*

*This is one of our favorite cookies. They are easy to make, tasty, and healthy too!*

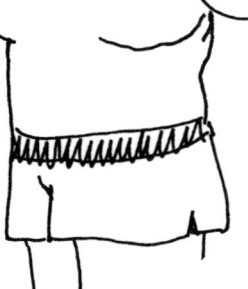

## SHORTBREAD

2 blocks butter or margarine
½ c. sugar
1 tsp. vanilla
2 c. flour

Cream together butter and sugar until light and fluffy. Add vanilla. Mix in flour. Pat into a 13 inch pan and bake at 325 degrees for 35-40 minutes or until golden in color. Poke holes in top after removing from oven, using fork. Cut into squares while still warm.

*A favorite at our house . . . very simple to make.*

## PUDDING BROWNIES

2 boxes chocolate or chocolate fudge pudding mix (not instant)
1 c. flour
½ tsp. baking powder
2/3 c. melted margarine
1¼ c. sugar
4 eggs
2 tsp. vanilla
1 c. chopped nuts (optional)

Mix together pudding, flour, and baking powder. Beat together margarine and sugar. Add eggs one at a time, beating well after each addition. Add the flour-pudding mixture to the margarine, sugar, and eggs. Add vanilla and chopped nuts last. Pour into a greased 13 inch pan and bake for 30 minutes at 350 degrees.   *24 bars*

*Tastier than brownie mix and almost as easy to make, this makes a large batch so freeze some for "desperation days."*

# WHEAT GERM PEANUT BARS

*This is a healthy dessert or breakfast bar.*

½ c. honey
½ c. butter or margarine
2 Tbsp. orange juice
2 eggs
1 tsp. vanilla
1 c. wheat germ
½ c. whole wheat flour
¼ tsp. baking soda
¾ c. chopped peanuts
1 egg white, lightly beaten

Cream butter and honey together until smooth. Beat in orange juice, eggs, vanilla. In another bowl stir together ¾ c. of the wheat germ, flour and baking soda. Add to butter mixture. Stir in ½ c. of the chopped peanuts. Press dough into a greased 10 x 6 inch pan. Brush top with egg white and sprinkle with the remaining wheat germ and chopped peanuts. Bake in 325 degree oven 25-30 minutes or until lightly browned.     *18 bars*

## MARBELOUS PEANUT BUTTER DESERT

Crust:
½ c. brown sugar
½ c. peanut butter
¼ c. margarine
1 c. flour

Mix all ingredients together and pat into a 13 inch pan. Bake for 15 minutes in 350 degree oven. Cool.

Filling:
8 oz. cream cheese
½ c. sugar
1 tsp. vanilla
2 eggs
1 small carton Cool Whip (8 oz.)

Beat all ingredients together until smooth. Pour over baked crust.

Topping:
½ c. semi-sweet chocolate bits melted over low heat. Drizzle melted chocolate over the filling. Take a knife and gently swirl the chocolate into the filling to create a "marble" effect.   *24 pieces*

Freeze at least 2 hours. Take out of freezer a few minutes before serving. Cut into squares.

## PEANUT BUTTER TREATS

*Especially for the peanut butter freaks.*

1 c. peanut butter
½ c. sugar
1 egg
4 oz. Baker's Sweet Chocolate

Mix peanut butter, sugar, and egg together until well blended. Press or roll dough into a 10 x 7 inch rectangle on an ungreased cookie sheet. Bake at 325 degrees for 20 minutes. Remove from oven and immediately arrange the chocolate on top and cover with aluminum foil until chocolate is melted. Remove aluminum foil. Spread melted chocolate over entire surface and immediately cut into 2 x 1 inch bars. Cool.   *30 bars*

## BANANA-GINGER LOAF

1 pkg. gingerbread mix
1 pkg. lemon instant pudding
1 c. milk
1 small carton of Cool Whip (8 oz.)
3 bananas
lemon or orange juice

Prepare gingerbread mix as stated on package. Bake in a greased and floured jelly roll pan (15½ x 10½ inches) for 20 minutes. (If you don't have a jelly roll pan, bake in 8 inch square pan). Remove from pan and cool on rack for 1 hour. Prepare instant pudding, using only 1 cup milk. Fold in Cool Whip. Cut the gingerbread into thirds. (If you used 8 inch pan cut into thirds horizontally). Thinly slice bananas and brush with lemon or orange juice to prevent discoloring. Place some banana slices on top of gingerbread; top with ½ of pudding mixture. Repeat with next layer. To serve, top with banana slices, overlapping them to create a neat appearance.   *Serves 6*

*This is another short cut recipe. Using convenience food is not a sin to me . . . makes cooking less of a hassle. And if it tastes good and is nutritous, why not?*

## OATMEAL BANANA CUPCAKES

½ c. white sugar
½ c. brown sugar (packed)
½ cup butter or margarine
2 eggs
3 medium bananas, mashed
1½ c. flour
1 tsp. baking powder
1 tsp. baking soda
½ tsp. salt
1 c. oatmeal

Cream together the sugars and butter. Beat in eggs and bananas. Stir in all other ingredients. Line 24 cupcake pans with paper liners. Spoon batter into pans and bake in 350 degree oven for 20 minutes. *24 cupcakes.*

## BANANA CREAM SQUARES

Crust:
2 blocks butter or margarine
2 Tbsp. sugar
2 c. flour

Blend ingredients well. Press into a 9 x 13 inch pan and bake at 325 degrees until golden brown. Line with sliced bananas (about 3 large).

Filling:
2 boxes vanilla instant pudding
1 8 oz. pkg. cream cheese
3 c. milk

Topping:
large container of Cool Whip

Mix the cream cheese with milk gradually until a smooth consistency is reached. Then add vanilla pudding and blend until thickened. Pour filling over bananas. Spread Cool Whip over filling. Refrigerate. Cut into squares.   *24 pieces*

Easy to prepare, this is another "impress your pals" dessert.

## BLUEBERRY CREAM CHEESE CAKE

Crust:
1½ blocks butter or margarine
1/3 c. brown sugar
1½ c. flour

Mix together and pat into a large pie pan or an 8 inch square pan. Bake 375 degrees for 15 minutes.

Filling:
1 box lemon jello
1 c. hot water
1 8 oz. pkg. cream cheese
1 c. sugar
1 large container of Cool Whip

Mix jello and hot water together. Cool. Blend together the cream cheese and sugar until smooth. Add the Cool Whip. Blend the jello and cream cheese mixture together. Pour into the baked crust. Refrigerate.

Topping:
1 can blueberry pie filling

Pour blueberry pie filling over top before serving. *Serves 6-8*

## SHORTBREAD PUMPKIN PIE

3 c. flour
½ c. sugar
1 c. margarine

Filling:
4 eggs, beaten
1 large can pumpkin
1 tsp. salt
1 tsp. cinnamon
1 tsp. ginger
1½ cups sugar
(or use 2 tsp. pumpkin pie spice instead of cinnamon and ginger)
2 cans evaporated milk (large cans)

You don't have to make a rolled crust for this pumpkin pie. It is a good one to make for a crowd.

Mix flour, sugar and margarine together and pat into a 13 inch pan. Mix filling in a large bowl. Pour over the crust and bake at 425 degrees for 20 minutes. Lower oven to 350 degrees and bake for 55 minutes.  *24 pieces*

## PEANUT-BANANA PIE

Prepared graham cracker crust

Filling:
1 pkg. vanilla pudding (not instant)
2 c. milk
¼ c. chunky peanut butter
3 medium bananas
Whipped cream or Cool Whip
chopped peanuts

Stir together pudding and milk. Add peanut butter and cook, stirring until mixture comes to a full boil. Cool 5 minutes, stirring twice. Slice the bananas into the prepared crust. Pour pudding over bananas. Cool. Serve with whipped cream or Cool Whip topped with chopped peanuts.
*Serves 6-8*

## APPLE PUDDING PIE

1 c. flour
1 c. sugar
1 tsp. baking soda
¼ tsp. nutmeg
¼ tsp. cinnamon
¼ c. melter butter or margarine
1 egg, beaten
2 c. finely chopped apples (about 2 medium)
½ c. chopped nuts (optional)

Mix together dry ingredients. Stir in butter, egg, apples, and nuts. Pour into a greased 9 inch pie pan. Bake at 350 degrees for 40-45 minutes. Sprinkle with powdered sugar and serve with ice cream.   Serves 6

*Not really a pie, this is a not too sweet, not too rich dessert.*

## APPLE CRISP

4-5 apples
¼ c. water
cinnamon to taste
1 cube margarine
1 c. brown sugar
1 c. flour
1 c. rolled oats (quick or old fashion)

Peel apples and slice thin. Place in an 8 inch pan. Pour water over apples and sprinkle with cinnamon. In a bowl combine margarine, brown sugar and flour. Cut the margarine into the dry ingredients so that the mixture is crumbly. Add oats. Pour crumb mixture over apples and pat gently.
Bake at 375 degrees for 35 minutes.

## DUMP CAKE

1 can prepared apple pie filling
2 c. flour
2 c. sugar
1 tsp. vanilla
2 tsp. baking soda
½ c. salad oil
1 tsp. cinnamon
2 eggs
1 c. chopped nuts

Mix all ingredients together. Beat 2-3 minutes with a portable mixer. Pour into a greased 9 x 13 inch pan. Bake at 325 degrees for 1 hour. Sprinkle top with powdered sugar when cool.   *24 pieces*

*If you can dump ingredients in a bowl, you can master this one.*

## OIL AND VINEGAR DRESSING

1 c. salad oil
¼ c. wine vinegar or cider vinegar
1 Tbsp. sugar
1 tsp. black pepper
2 tsp. salt
1¼ tsp. paprika
1 tsp. grated onion
3 Tbsp. water

Shake all ingredients together in a jar.

*To this basic dressing you can add herbs, Parmesan cheese, or minced garlic for a different flavor.*

## FAVORITE FRENCH DRESSING

¼ c. sugar
dash of pepper
½ tsp. salt
½ c. catsup
¾ c. salad oil
¼ c. cider vinegar
¼ c. finely chopped onion
1 clove finely chopped garlic, if desired

Combine all ingredients in a jar. Shake well.

## EASY GARLIC BREAD

Buy sliced French bread. Spread with butter or margarine. Sprinkle with garlic salt, Parmesan cheese, and paprika. Place under broiler for a few minutes until lightly browned. Watch carefully because it burns easily!

## ROQUEFORT DRESSING

2 c. mayonnaise
1 c. sour cream
2 cloves garlic, mashed
1/3 c. vinegar
2 Tbsp. lemon juice
½ lb. Roquefort cheese, crumbled
(Blue cheese may be substituted)

Mix all ingredients together. Pour into a jar. This dressing keeps several weeks in the refrigerator.

# FRUIT FRENCH DRESSING

1/3 c. sugar
1 tsp. salt
1 tsp. paprika
juice of 1 lemon
juice of 1 orange
1 Tbsp. vinegar
1 c. oil
1 tsp. grated onion

Shake all ingredients in a jar. Makes 1¾ cups.

*Use on either green salad or fruit salad. It is a light refreshing dressing.*
*Yield: 1¾ cups*

# GUACAMOLE

2 ripe avocados, mashed
1 Tbsp. mayonnaise
3 Tbsp. lemon juice
2 Tbsp. finely minced onion
½ tsp. salt
3-4 drops hot sauce
1 tomato, finely chopped (optional)

Mix all ingredients together.
Cover and chill. Serve with tortilla chips. *Serves 4-6*

*Garnish this dip with chopped Chinese parsley (cilantro or coriander).*

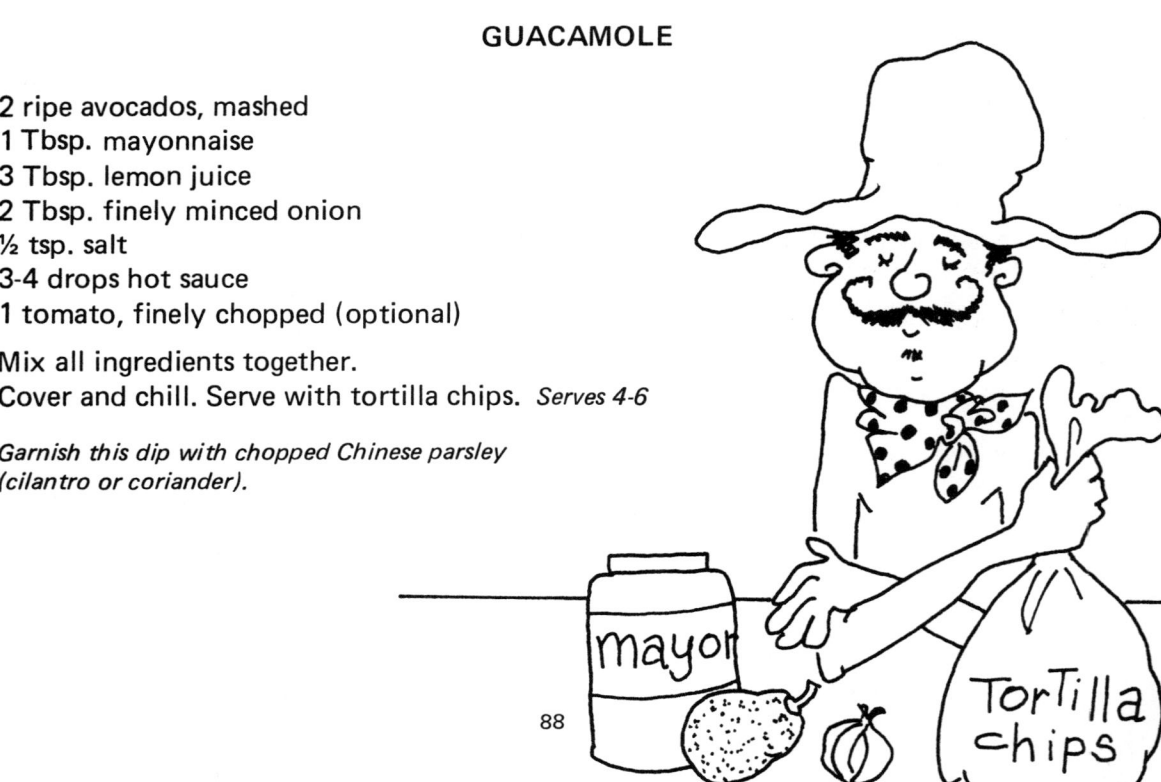

# CHILI DIP

*Especially good with tortilla chips!*

1 8 oz. pkg. cream cheese
½ c. mayonnaise
½ c. cottage cheese
½ tsp. garlic salt
1 small can chopped green chilies (if you use hot chilies, do not use entire can)
2 Tbsp. chives or green onions, chopped

Mix all ingredients together and chill.
Use as a dip for chips or vegies.

## VINAIGRETTE VEGIES

1 c. salad oil
5 Tbsp. vinegar (cider or wine)
1½ tsp. dry oregano
1 tsp. salt
½ tsp. pepper
2 cloves garlic, minced

Vegies:
Thick slices of tomatoes, cucumber, or zucchini, green pepper, cauliflower, sliced mushrooms, or carrots.

Mix dressing ingredients together in a covered container. Marinate vegies in dressing 2-3 hours in refrigerator. Serve on crisp lettuce. Any leftover dressing may be used to marinate steak, or more vegies.

## MACARONI SALAD

½ pkg. salad macaroni, cooked in salted water and drained
2 Tbsp. finely minced onion
1 c. finely diced celery
1 carrot, finely minced
1 small can sliced olives
1-1½ c. cheddar cheese, diced
1/3 c. sweet pickle relish
1 Tbsp. sugar
¾ tsp. salt
½ tsp. pepper
mayonnaise—enough to moisten the ingredients
3 hard boiled eggs, sliced

Mix all ingredients, except eggs together.
Chill. Garnish with sliced hard boiled eggs. *Serves 6-8*

*Cheese, olives, and eggs make this a pretty salad.*

# BARBEQUE SAUCE

1 envelope dry onion soup mix
1 c. chili sauce
½ c. brown sugar
¼ c. lemon juice
1 Tbsp. prepared mustard
1½ c. water

Combine and simmer 20 minutes.
Use on chicken, hamburgers, steaks, etc.
Leftover sauce may be kept in refrigerator.

*A versatile sauce that gives zing to plain old every day food.*

## DILLY DIP

1 c. sour cream
½ c. mayonnaise
1 tsp. dill weed
1 Tbsp. prepared mustard
½ to 1 tsp. salt

Mix all ingredients together. Serve with chips or fresh raw vegetables such as carrots, celery, cauliflower, cucumbers, etc.

## POPEYE DIP

1 (9 oz.) pkg. creamed spinach, thawed
2 c. mayonnaise
1 tsp. salt
¼ c. instant minced onion flakes
¼ c. parsley flakes

Combine all ingredients together in a bowl. Cover and refrigerate. Serve with crisp vegies or crackers.

# Helpful Hints

**HELPFUL HINTS:**

Good items to keep on hand for "desperation food" include:
In refrigerator or freezer:
> hot dogs
> hamburger
> eggs
> peas and carrots

Note: hamburger, even if frozen, will thaw quickly over a low heat.

On the shelf: tuna, beans, canned chicken, cream of mushroom soup, corned beef, noodles, or macaroni

**COMPARSION SHOPPING:**
Learn to compare prices at the market. Sometimes the cheaper brand may not look as pretty, but if you're going to make soup or sauce out of it, looks don't matter.

**CLEAR UP AS YOU GO:**
Try to clean up as you cook. Washing and putting away dishes and utensils you won't need again makes dishwashing after the meal easier.

**WASHING DISHES:**
If you have to wash dishes by hand, wash the cleanest ones first. For example, wash glasses and silverware first, pots and pans last.

**CHEAP CONTAINERS:**
Save jars and plastic containers. You can store leftovers in them, shake sauces and salad dressing in them, and later throw away (no washing!).

**GETTING RID OF GREASE:**
Don't pour oil or grease down the drain. Pour it in a jar or can with cover (after oil is cool) and toss it in the trash.

**BLACK CAST IRON SKILLET:**
The old fashioned black cast iron skillet is a most useful pan. It conducts heat evenly and well, and its surface doesn't scratch with scouring. It can be used for everything from frying eggs to cooking stir-fry Chinese dishes.
Be sure you "season" a new pan. To do this, heat cooking oil in it. Also rub oil on its outer surface. After a few "seasoning sessions" the black pan is ready for use. Wash it in warm water and detergent after each use, and be sure to dry it or it will rust. Do not put it in the dishwasher!

**MAKING THE RECIPE FIT:**
Some of the recipes included in this book make a large quantity. Either make these dishes for company, or put uncooked portions in small foil pans and freeze for another meal or two, or you can put your mathmatical skills to work and divide the recipe to suit your needs.

**MENU PLANNING:**
Try to plan your menu around foods that are "on special" at the market. For example, if chicken is cheap, make one of the chicken recipes . . . or buy a couple of chickens and freeze them for future use.

**SERVINGS:**
Servings stated in this book are only approximate. They are generous servings for hearty eaters.

**PERSONALIZE RECIPES:**
Cooking is very personal. These recipes do not have to be adhered to rigidly. Take them as a starting point. As you gain experience, you will be able to add or delete according to your personal preference.

## ORIENTAL RICE:
To cook Oriental rice (Calrose) in a pot on the stove: Measure rice into a pan with a cover. Rinse rice twice. To each cup of rice use 1 c. water. Bring rice to a boil (covered) on high heat. Turn stove down to lowest point (simmer) for 20 minutes. Turn off heat. Let rice sit in the pan for at least 15 more minutes. Rice will stick to the bottom of the pan if removed immediately. 1 cup of uncooked rice will serve 3 average eaters or 2 with hefty appetites.

## LEFTOVER RICE:
Do not throw away leftover rice. Keep it in the freezer, wrapped in foil. When you have enough leftover, make fried rice. Leftover rice makes better fried rice than freshly cooked rice.

## BAKING POTATOES:
To bake a potato: Wash it well. Bake in a 400 degree oven for 45 minutes, or at a lower temperature for a longer time.

## MINCED ONION:
Keep instant minced onions on your shelf to use when you don't have a fresh onion on hand. 1 Tbsp. instant minced onion equals 1 small onion.

## GARLIC & GINGER ROOT:
Garlic and ginger root freeze well. If you don't use these often, keep them in a plastic bag in the freezer.

## HOW TO USE ROUND STEAK:
Lean cuts of beef such as round steak are cheaper and better for your health (less fat). Round steak can be broiled—do not overcook. Slice it in thin diagonal strips and sprinkle with garlic salt, or serve with sauces such as barbeque or teriyaki sauce.

## TORTILLAS:
To heat tortillas: Wrap in foil and heat in a 350 degree oven for about 15 minutes.

**EQUIVALENTS**

3 teaspoons = 1 Tablespoon
4 Tablespoons = ¼ cup
2 cups = 1 pint = .473 liters
4 cups = 2 pints = 1 quart = .946 liters
4 quarts = 1 gallon = 3.785 liters
½ cup butter or margarine = 1 stick or ¼ pound

**MEASURING DRY INGREDIENTS:**
To measure dry ingredients in a measuring cup, dip the cup into the flour (or whatever you are measuring) and fill it lightly. Level top with a knife. The only exception is brown sugar. This should be packed into the cup.

**MEASURING SHORTENING:**
To measure shortening or butter in a measuring cup, pack it in so that no air pockets exist. Level top with a rubber spatula.

## NECESSARY EQUIPMENT FOR COOKING

You will want to add to this basic list as you become a more experienced cook.

Baking Pans:
8 inch square pan
13 X 9 inch oblong pan
9 inch loaf pan
cupcake pan
cookie sheets

Note: If you don't bake a lot and don't want to invest in baking pans, you may want to buy disposable foil pans as needed.

Chopping Board: Wooden or plastic.

Colander: This looks like a bowl with holes in it for draining foods such as pasta. It can be made out of metal or plastic.

Cooking Fork: Larger than a normal fork, with a longer handle.

## NECESSARY EQUIPMENT FOR COOKING

Egg Beater: Hand beater is a necessity. If you plan to bake a lot, get an electric portable model.

Grater: Get one that grates fine, medium, and coarse.

Juicer: Made out of plastic, metal, or glass, this item is necessary for squeezing lemon or orange juice.

Knives: One 8 or 9 inch all-purpose knife and a paring knife are essentials.

Ladle: This utensil has a deep bowl so you can scoop up soups, sauces, gravies, etc.

Measuring Cups: 1 set for dry ingredients; graduated set of ¼ cup, 1/3 cup. ½ cup, and 1 cup. For liquid ingredients get a 1 cup size with graduations made out of glass or plastic. A 1 quart size is useful, but not essential.

## NECESSARY EQUIPMENT FOR COOKING

Measuring Spoons: 1 set in standard sizes of ¼ tsp., ½ tsp., 1 tsp., and 1 Tbsp.

Metal Spatula: For turning foods over and for removing food from pans.

Mixing Bowls: Get a set of three—small, medium, and large made out of glass or stainless steel.

Openers: Essentials are a bottle opener, corkscrew, and a beer can opener. A heavy duty can opener (manual or electric) is also necessary.

Rubber Spatula or Scraper: Scrapes a bowl clean -without using your hand!

Saucepans with lids:
Small (1-2 cups)
Medium (2 quarts)
Large (8 quarts)
Heavy oven-proof stew pot, Dutch oven, or covered casserole.

## NECESSARY EQUIPMENT FOR COOKING

Skillets: Black cast iron skillet (10 inches) for all purpose use.
Large (10 inch) skillet with a cover (or electric skillet).
Smaller skillet (6-7 inches) for cooking eggs or heating leftovers.

Strainer: A medium sized one is essential.

Timer: Most stoves come with a timer. If yours does not, get a free standing one.

Tongs: Use these for turning foods without piercing them.

Vegetable Peeler: Essential for peeling fruit and vegetables.

Whisk: A utensil with many strands of wire looped to form a balloon-like shape on a handle. Good for beating and for making gravy and sauce without lumps.

## NECESSARY EQUIPMENT FOR COOKING

Wire cooling rack: For cooling cookies, cakes, etc.

Wooden spoons: Good for all purpose spoon in cooking; you'll probably want more than one.

## TYPES OF LETTUCE

Head Lettuce: Also known as iceberg lettuce; leaves are light green in color.

Romaine: A long leaf lettuce; dark green in color and crunchy.

Butter Lettuce: A loose-leafed lettuce; tender, delicate flavor.

Manoa Lettuce: Grown in Hawaii, similar to butter lettuce, but leaves are darker green and crisp.

Red Leaf Lettuce: A loose-leafed lettuce with leaves tinged red. Adds nice color.

Leaf Lettuce: Has curly tipped loose leaves. Bright green in color and tender texture.

## EASY MENUS FOR FUN ENTERTAINING

### IMPRESS YOUR COMPANY DINNER

Green Salad with Fruit French Dressing
Short Cut Beef Stroganoff
Hot Rice or Noodles
Buttered Peas (frozen)
Peanut-Banana Pie

### SUNDAY BRUNCH

Fresh Fruit (use whatever is in season, cut
    it up and arrange attractively on platter)
Huevos Rancheros
Warm Tortillas
Milk or Coffee

### JAPANESE DINNER

Cucumber Namasu
Sukiyaki
Hot Rice
Takuwan
Cream Cheese Kanten
Hot Tea

### HAWAIIAN PICNIC

Cucumber Namasu
Baked Teriyaki Chicken
Oriental Omelet
Easy Pan Sushi
Takuwan
Pineapple Squares

### MEXICAN PARTY

Guacamole with Chips
Vinaigrette Vegies
Chalupa
Hot Tortillas
Apple Pudding Pie

## BASIC HAMBURGER/MEATBALL MIX

1 lb. ground beef
½ small onion, chopped
1 egg
¼ c. catsup
1 slice bread, crumbled
1 tsp. salt
½ tsp. pepper

Mix all ingredients together and form into patties or meatballs.

Note: Canned tomato or cream of mushroom soup (undiluted) may be poured over raw meatballs and baked for about 1 hour in 350 degree oven. Or, you may brown the meatballs in a pan and pour sweet-sour, barbecue, or teriyaki sauce over them.

# BASIC CREAM SAUCE

¼ c. butter or margarine
3 Tbsp. flour
2 c. milk
salt and pepper to taste

Melt butter or margarine in a saucepan. Add flour and blend together. Add milk slowly. Cook until thick over medium heat, stirring constantly.

To this sauce you can add canned tuna, chicken, salmon, etc.

For cheese sauce: add 1 c. grated cheese.

**HOW TO BOIL A CHICKEN:**

Many recipes call for cooked, boned chicken. You may use a fryer, roaster, or chicken parts. Put the chicken in a large pot with a cover. Cover the chicken with water. Add 1½ tsp. salt and a cut up onion. Bring the water to a boil; turn down heat to simmer. Cover and cook chicken for 45 minutes (30 minutes if you use cut up chicken).

Remove chicken from broth and cool. After it is cool enough to handle, remove skin and bones. Cut or shred chicken into bite-size pieces.

**HOW TO THICKEN GRAVY**

Add water to pan juices to make about 2-2½ cups liquid. Put ½ cup water in a jar or covered container. Add to it 3 Tbsp. flour. Shake well—should be the consistency of white glue. Add this mixture gradually to the pan juices until desired consistency is reached.
This same flour-water mixture can be used to thicken stew.
Be sure to add it slowly and stop when desired consistency is reached.

# GLOSSARY

Bamboo shoots: Tender shoots of the bamboo plant. Sold in cans, packed in water. Available in Hawaii markets and some Oriental food sections of mainland markets.

Basil: Herb with a spicy aroma. Often used in sauces and soups; an essential ingredient in many French, Italian, and Greek dishes.

Beat: To mix quickly, incorporating as much air as possible to make a mixture light and smooth.

Boullion: A broth made by simmering meat in liquid. May be bought in concentrated cubes or crystals.

Brown: To cook meat over moderately high heat quickly in order to seal in the juices.

Chilies: Green chili pepper; available in cans, packed in brine. Available in mild or hot varieties. Use hot chilies sparingly.

Chinese Parsley: Also known as cilantro or coriander, it is used as a flavoring and garnish in Chinese and Mexican dishes.

Chives: Mild member of the onion family; only the green, flat leaves are used for seasoning. Easily grown in a pot.

Cilantro: See Chinese Parsley.

Chop: To cut into small pieces with a knife, food chopper, or processor.

Coriander: See Chinese Parsley.

Cream: To work foods together until soft and blended, i. e., creaming butter and sugar together.

# GLOSSARY

Crepes: Thin French pancakes stuffed with fillings. May be either a main dish or dessert.

Cumin: A spice often used in Mexican dishes; resembles caraway in odor and flavor.

Dice: To cut into approximately ¼ inch cubes.

Fold: To incorporate any airy substance such as whipped cream or egg whites into a heavier substance. The purpose of folding is to retain volume. To fold, use a rubber spatula to cut through the substance and turn it over until well blended.

Fry: To cook in a skillet with some fat or oil. Pan frying requires a small amount of oil or fat while deep frying requires 3-4 cups of hot fat or oil.

Grease (a pan): To cover surface of a pan with a coating of shortening or butter so that foods will not stick. (Spray on pan coating may be used in place of shortening or butter).

Guacamole: Avocado dip, usually eaten in Mexico as an appetizer with tortillas or other snacks such as crisp pork rind and crisp-fried tortillas.

Ginger: Root of a tropical plant used in Oriental dishes. Sold in markets in Hawaii and some specialty markets on the mainland. If not available, substitute 1 tsp. bottled, dry ginger.
A one inch piece of ginger root.

Guava: Tart tropical fruit. Largely pulp and seed, it is consequently made into juice or jam and jelly.

# GLOSSARY

Hawaiian Salt: Also known as rock salt. Common salt of large, coarse crystals.

Huevo: egg (Spanish)

Huevos Rancheros: Spanish for eggs, country style; litterally, "of the ranch."

Julienne: To cut into thin, match-stick like strips. To julienne, make a stack of 1/8 inch slices, than cut down at 1/8 intervals.

Kalua Pig: Hawaiian style roast pork; traditionally cooked in an underground oven called an imu.

Kanten: Japanese gelatin dessert made from seaweed (agar agar).

Kim Chee: Korean pickled vegetables flavored with garlic and red pepper.

Laulau: Hawaiian dish; bundle of meat (usually pork) wrapped in ti leaves and steamed.

Lentils: Greenish-brown, flat beans; high in protein. More digestible than animal protein.

Liquid Smoke: Smoke flavor in a bottle. Use only when you cannot achieve natural smoke flavor.

Long Rice: Also known as "cellophane noodles." Transparent noodles made out of mung bean starch; used in Oriental dishes. Must be softened in water before use. Available in Hawaii markets and some oriental food sections of mainland markets.

Luau Leaves: Green leaves of the taro plant: used as a green vegetable.

Macadamia Nuts: Crisp, white nuts commercially cultivated in Hawaii. Sold salted, in cans, or in bits for baking.

## GLOSSARY

Mandarin Orange: Tangerine sections with membranes removed; sold in cans.

Malasadas: Portuguese doughnuts.

Marinate: To cover foods with seasoned sauce or other liquid in order to allow the flavor of the sauce to soak in.

Marjoram: A versatile herb with a sweet, spicy flavor.

Nutmeg: A spice obtained from the fruit of a tree, *Myristica fragrans,* a native of Indonesia. Nutmeg is used mostly for flavoring in deserts and certain vegetables and sauces.

Oregano: Herb also known as wild marjoram; often used in Italian, Spanish, and Mexican dishes.

Pepperoni: Spicy Italian sausage.

Pupu: Hawaiian word for appetizer.

Rice, Calrose: A medium grain rice preferred by Orientals. Tends to be more moist than long grain rice.

Saute: To cook gently on top of stove, using less fat and heat than in frying.

Score: To make shallow cuts with a knife blade about ½ to ¾ inch apart.

Sesame Oil: Also known as Goma Oil. Oil of sesame seeds. Has a distinctive aroma and is used in many Oriental foods.

Sesame Seed: Small white seeds that give a nutty flavor and distinctive aroma to foods. Often used in Oriental cooking. To get ultimate flavor and aroma, toast the seeds

## GLOSSARY

in an ungreased pan over high heat until brown. Then break the skins of the seeds with a mortar and pestal or the back of a spoon.

Shoyu: Also known as soy sauce, it is a key seasoning in Japanese (and other Oriental) cooking.

Shred: To cut or tear into thin strips.

Simmer: To boil very gently. The liquid should barely bubble.

Souffle: A light, fluffy baked dish made with eggs.

Stir: To blend briskly with a spoon in a circular motion.

Stir-Fry: Method of cooking meats and vegetables quickly over high heat in a small amount of oil, agitating or stirring the food as it cooks. Used to prepare many Oriental dishes.

Sushi: Rice flavored with vinegar sauce; a Japanese dish.

Takuwan: Japanese pickled turnip. Often eaten at the end of a meal with rice and tea.

Tofu: Soybean curd; white and custard-like in appearance. May be eaten plain or cooked with other ingredients. High in protein.

Tortilla: Thin pancake of ground corn or flour. (Mexican).

Water Chestnuts: Tuber of a plant (sledge) which grows in shallow water. Sold fresh in Hawaii markets and in some Oriental food markets on mainland, but usually found in cans, peeled and packed in water. It is used mainly for its crunchy texture rather than for its flavor in Oriental cooking.

# INDEX

Apple Crisp, 81
Apple Pudding Pie, 80
Baked Fish, 24
Baked Teriyaki Chicken, 43
Baking Potatoes, 89
Banana Cream Squares, 76
Banana Ginger Loaf, 74
Barbeque Sauce, 92
Beanie-Weenies, 60
Beef Curry, 49
Beef with Vegetables, 40
Beer-be-cued Chicken, 18
Blueberry Cream Cheese Cake, 77
Chalupa, 15
Cheap containers, 97
Cheese Sauce, 109
Chicken Diable, 16
Chicken, How to Boil, 110
Chicken Noodle Casserole, 62
Chicken with Vegetables, 40
Chili Dog, 89
Chinese Salad, 30
Citrus Pineapple Loaf, 54

# INDEX

Company Stew, 6
Comparision shopping, 96
Confetti Corned Beef, 64
Corned Beef Hash Patties, 58
Cream Cheese Kanten, 55
Creamed Tuna, 61
Desperation foods, 96
Dilly Dip, 93
Dump Cake, 82
Easy Cheesy Chicken, 17
Easy Chili, 7
Easy Garlic Bread, 85
Easy Pan Sushi, 44
Easy Pot Roast, 20
Enchilada Casserole, 10
Equipment, 97; 101-105
Equivalents, 100
Favorite French Dressing, 85
Fried Rice, 35
Fruit French Dressing, 87
Garlic, 99
Ginger Root, 99
Grandma's Takuwan, 32

# INDEX

Gravy, How to Thicken, 110
Grease, Getting Rid of, 97
Guava Crsipies, 51
Guacamole, 88
Hamburger/Meatball Mix, 108
Hawaiian Cream Cheese Spread, 33
Healthy Cookies, 68
Huevos Rancheros, 12
Korean Barbeque Sauce, 34
Lentil Vegetable Soup, 4
Lettuce, Types of, 106
Macadamia Butter Bars, 53
Macaroni Salad, 91
Marbelous Peanut Butter Desert, 72
Measuring, 100;
   Dry ingredients, 100;
   shortening, 100
Meat Loaf, 19
Menus, 107
Mexican Chef's Salad, 13
Mexican Chicken Crepes, 14
Mickey's Hamburger Stroganoff, 22
Mickey's Mor 's Chili Rellenos, 11

# INDEX

Minced Onion, 99
Minute Steak-Oriental Style, 4
Mock Malasadas, 50
Mock Laulau, 47
Namasu (vinegared vegetables), 31
Oatmeal Banana Cupcakes, 75
Oil and Vinegar Dressing, 84
Oriental Omelet, 36
Oriental Rice, 99
Oven Kalua Pig, 48
Peanut-Banana Pie, 79
Peanut Butter Treats, 73
Pepperoni Soup, 2
Pineapple-Banana Smoothie, 56
Pineapple Squares, 52
Pizza Sandwich Spread, 9
Popeye Dip, 94
Popping Peas, 23
Pudding Brownies, 70
Quick Beef Chowder, 5
Quick & Easy Kim Chee Salad, 29
Rice:
    Fried, 35

# INDEX

    Left over, 99;
    Oriental, 99
Roquefort Dressing, 86
Round Steak, 99
Scrambled Eggs, 59
Scrambled Hamburgers, 63
Short Bread, 69
Short Bread Pumpkin Pie, 78
Short Cut Beef Stroganoff, 21
Spaghetti Sauce, 8
Sukiyaki, 39
Sweet Sour Chicken, 37
Sweet Sour Spareribs, 38
Sweet Sour Tofu & Vegetables, 46
Teri-Hot Dogs, 61
Teriyaki Chicken or Beef on a Stick,
    42
Tofu Patties, 45
Tortillas, 99
Tuna Burgers, 25
Tuna Souffle, 26
Vinaigarette Vegies, 90
Wheat Germ Peanut Bars, 71

# NOTES

# NOTES

# NOTES

# NOTES

# NOTES